Fortune Cookies

Volume 2

Dr. Kareem Pottinger

YSD Publishing House

Library of Congress Catalog in Publication Data

Copyright 2007 by KAREEM POTTINGER

YSD PUBLISHING HOUSE
14490 Coastal Bay Circle 13204
Naples, FL. 34119

Library of Congress Catalog Card Number:
2013934185
International Standard Book Number 978-1-937171-01-8

Dedicated to my firstborn

YOUNGSABATH POTTINGER

If I ever leave this planet, I have always kept you in mind.

Not leavening my wisdom far behind

Grow Good

INTRODUCTION

The true intent of this book
was to write a set of guidelines
that could be
immediately implemented in
the progress and advancement
of my sons elite
life.
This vast deep knowledge was
to be used as a
tool
to keep him far beyond just,
"ahead of the learning curb" for
lack of better expression.
These
rules are the widely accepted
and used unspoken
secrets amongst the elite in
which we use to rear our

young.
Although these are our
secrets
and most of us will and should
be extremely displeased for
having them on display for the
"normal's" of the world to
receive, I decided to release
them nevertheless.
For,
upon reading the finished
piece I realized that these elite
secrets
could not only serve to benefit
my son and family to come
well, but that the entire
world
could serve to benefit from
these lists of guidelines.
The way that this book is
intended to be received is to

ponder upon each page for a
complete 24 hours.
Each page is to be pondered
upon for the whole day; it is to
be used as topic of discussion
for that day amongst peers,
friends, and family members'
etcetera.
It is especially designed to be
pondered upon mostly by you.
For a complete 24 hours deep
thought on each subject
should be pondered upon. The
reason being is to see how
these guidelines could
be
implemented into your current
life,
how should they have been
implemented in your past
life, and how can they benefit
your future.

It
is only through the true
belief
and usage of these
guidelines
that your life's
works will be greatly
affected
in its progress.

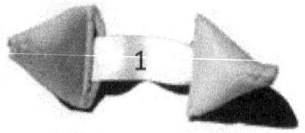

*Money will
always
have a
way
of
making
people
reasonable
once
you have
learnt how to
use it*

*Like
the
people
you like
and do not
like
the people
you
don't;
it's
for a
reason*

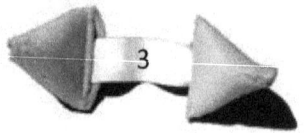

When you are
always
dwelling upon
the offence,
it makes
it
harder
for you
to
forgive
that
offence

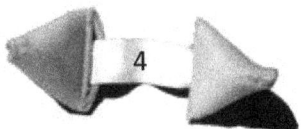

*When
unexpected
things pop-up,
most times
it is
best to
improvise
rather than
to
continue
with your
original-plan*

*Being
spontaneous
is the
thing
that
builds
the
youth
which
keeps
you
young*

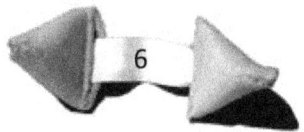

The greatest asset that a person can have is someone who believes in them

*Do not ever
let
someone
else
convince
you
that you
have
seen
enough
in
life*

You have too
want
the destiny that
you would like
to live in
life
so bad
that you
are not
afraid
to go
after it

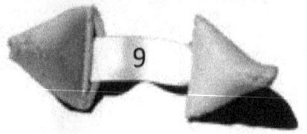

*Sometimes
when you brace
yourself
for a
bumpy
ride,
you get
surprised
of how
the
roads
clear-up*

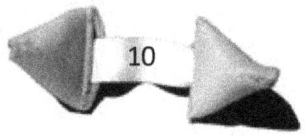

*Doing the
right-thing
for yourself
will
always
make you
feel-great
so
start doing
more of the
right-thing
for yourself*

*When
you
have
to
much
of
everything
your
bound
to
lose
something*

*Your sense
of right
from
wrong
might not
be
their
same-sense
of
right
from
wrong*

*Whenever
you
screw-up
know
that
you may now
have to
do something
that you do not
want too
in order to
fix it*

*Anything
that
is
not
moving
forward
in
life
is
moving
backwards*

*Everything
makes
perfect
sense
to
everyone
until
they
have
to
pay*

*Your
old-problems
will compound
your
new-problems
which
is why it is very
important to fix
all your
problems as
soon as
possible*

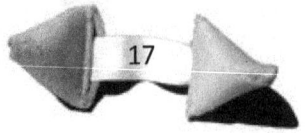

Good
business
is
where
you
will
always
find
money

*Judge
a
person
by
how they
act
and not
by
what
they
tell
you*

*When you
have
a
dream
it
will
always
be
up to
you
to
protect-it*

*When you
continue
to put
in
work
into
your
efforts
change
will
come
eventually*

You should never throw good money after bad money

Receiving
too
much
of
what
nourishes
you
can
begin
to
deplete
you

*When
something
does not feel
right,
there
is
usually
something
that
is
false
there*

When
you are
true
in
your
efforts
the
universe
will
lift
you
up

*A
minor
setback
can
work
towards
a
major
comeback*

*In life
it's extremely
important
that you
look,
listen,
and
observe
more
than
you
speak*

You will be
unable to
blossom
into your
fullest potential
if you are
unwilling to
venture
of into
unknown
or
new territory

*Just
because you
share a
laugh with an
individual
doesn't mean
that the
individual
isn't
an
unsavory
character*

*Why
take the
risk
if
you
have
already
taken-one,
should
be
your
question*

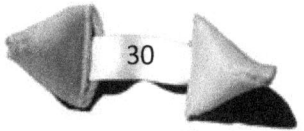

The very moment that you realize you are stalling out is the same time that you need to refocus your aim

*Life's
a
beach
so
watch
out
for
the
crabs*

*If you have to
ask,
then the
answer
must
be
no
because
if it were yes
you wouldn't
have to
ask*

*From
the
fool
you
realize
how
not
to
become
a
fool*

*You
should
never
turn
down
an
opportunity
to
better
yourself*

*Life
is
all
about
the
problem,
the
solution,
and
the
answer*

Whenever you say enough is enough, then that is where your line is drawn

*Anything
that
you do
for a long
period of time
you can become
bored of
unless
you
really are in
love
with it*

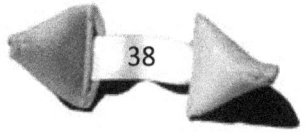

In
order
to
succeed
you
cannot
be
afraid
to
fail

All things
have
a
destiny
and your
destiny
will be
set into
place
depending
upon
your-actions

*Through
competition
we
can
discover
our
true
selves*

*In life
no-one
can
guarantee
that
things
are
always
going
to
be
fair*

You should always try to meet and learn from the best

*You are
your
own
angel
and
you can
also
very well
become
your
own
demon*

*Do
not
preach
anything
you do not
practice
or
run the risk
of
becoming
a
hypocrite*

*The
heart
is
born
with
the
knowledge
of
right
from
wrong*

The experiences that you live through in life make you who you are

*You
can't
really
change
that
which
is
truly
in
another
person's
heart*

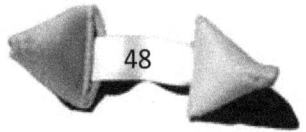

*It's
ironic
how
the
truth
sometimes
is a lot
harder
to
absorb
than a
lie*

*Not
one
of
us
acts
exactly
the
same
in
front
of
everyone*

*Starting
a business
is a
risk;
if not, then
you
did
not
start
the
right
business*

*Do not
get
so
enthralled
in
the
lesser-good
that
you
miss-out
on the
greater-good*

*The only thing
that you can
count
on in this world
is the
fact that
people
are
going
to
make
mistakes*

*Always
remember
that a
smaller-portion
of a
big thing
is a lot
better
than a
big-portion
of a
small thing*

*Sometimes
you
can
tell
how
a
person's
story
will end
by
how
it begins*

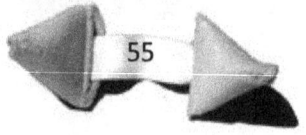

When something that was once ritual becomes habitual, then it is a problem

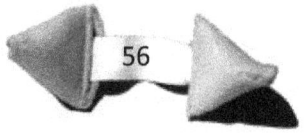

*No-one
comes and
improves
your
life
for you,
you have to
come to terms
with this
and improve
your life
yourself*

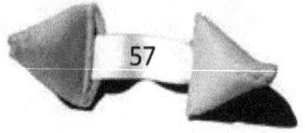

It's one thing
to look
at the
grey spaces
in
the world
it is
a totally
different thing
living
in
them

*You
should
never
trust
the
people
who
are
not
to
be
trusted*

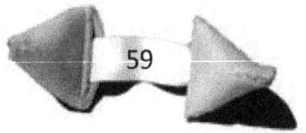

*Never
let
anything
hold
you
back
from
accomplishing
your
goals*

*Certain reality
is hidden
for
a
reason
which is why
you should
pick
your spots
carefully
if you are to
avail-it*

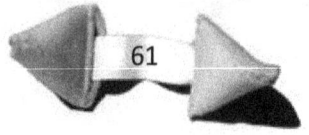

You cannot connect the dots until you collect the dots

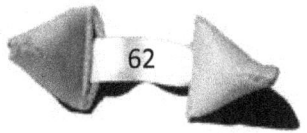

*Only
take
people
as they
are,
not
for
what
you
think
they're
worth*

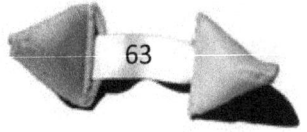

*In order
to
defeat
your
assailant
you
must
first
take
care
of
yourself*

*What
you think
people are
worth
and what
their
true-value
is equaled to
usually
never
adds
up*

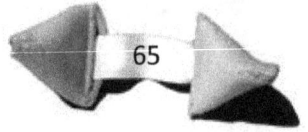

*Every
profession
has
its
occupational
hazards*

*You
never
know
how long
anything
will last
so
you should
always
take
full
advantage*

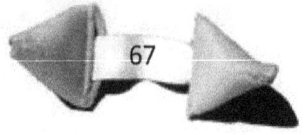

You have
yourself
and
most
of
the
time
that is
all
that
you will
need

*It
will
always
work
to
your
benefit
for
you
not to
lose
your-calm*

*Sometimes
if you
give
people
a week
they
might
change
the way
that
they
feel*

The most problem with people is that their small, they have never done anything big their whole entire life; they think small, live small, and dream small

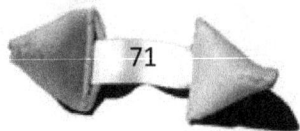

Take chances

You
should
always
do
what
makes
sense
for
you
too
do

*Do
not
get
fooled
by
a
manipulators
tears*

*If
you
are
not
careful
life
will
pass
you
by
extremely
fast*

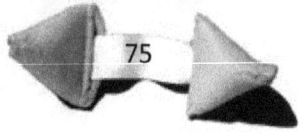

*Stay
focused
on
your
goal
and
one
day
you
will
achieve
it*

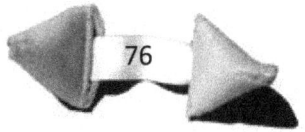

You should always keep in mind that what you are seeing visually may only be a part of what is truly happening

*In
anything
that
you are
really
trying to
accomplish
you
have to
have
a
strategy*

*A winner
gets
up
off
of
their
behinds
in order
to
perform
so that they
can win*

*You
should
never
be
big
on
giving-out
your
opinion*

Having money is easier

*In
life
you
should
refuse
not
to
give
yourself
what
you
want*

There
is
nothing wrong
with trying
and
failing
but to
try and then
give-up, will
never
be
respected

*Make
sure
that
no-one
in
your
circle
falls
of
that
tight
rope*

When
you are
not
on
firm
footing
your
main-purpose
should
be
getting
some

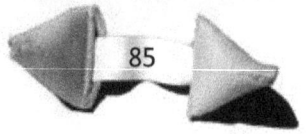

*Getting a
normal job
and being
normal
is for
normal people
so your
main question
should be
are
you
normal*

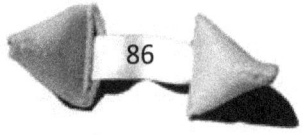

*At the end
of it
all, you'll
overlook
a lot of
mistakes
when the task
that you were
trying to
accomplish
turns-out
great*

Prefer
to
leap over
the
bar of approval
and
not
just too
just
walk
underneath
it

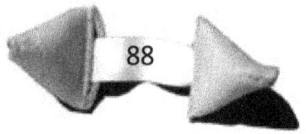

When

you

are

better

there

is

no

need

to

compete

*Loners
keep
themselves
good
company
which
is why
they
prefer
to
be
alone*

*It is only
one-life that we
as human
beings get and
know so*

you

should

really

do

your

best

each-day

*In this short life
span
of ours
there is a lot
that you
should
want to see
and
do
so don't
waste any
time of it, at all*

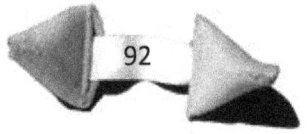

*Always
remember that
the people
who are
ahead of you
already
know
what
they are
going
to do
next*

*Just because
you have
received
help from
a
person
does not
mean
that
person is
your
friend*

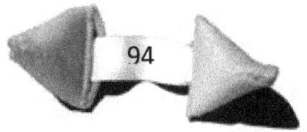

*You
should
never
presume
to
know
what
other
people
think
or
feel*

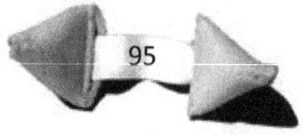

Any great task
ever
accomplished
always
started
out
as
a
vision
and
a
dream

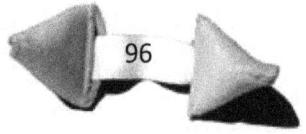

Only

a

fool

would

bet on

a

horse

to

win

a

football

game

*When
it is time
to serve
your
purpose
don't
ask
questions
just
serve
your
purpose*

*Whatever
you choose
to do in
life
will only
turn-out
great
when
you put
your
all
into it*

*In order
to
compound
your
popularity
you have to
surround
yourself around
people
that
are
popular*

*If
it's out
there for
you to
reach-it
and
grab-it,
then go
right ahead
and
consume
it*

*There
are
no
free
rides
on
the
road
to
success*

*Nothings
to
beautiful
or
expensive
for you
to
obtain
should always
be
your
attitude*

Regroup and figure out what you are strongest in, then consistently aim a little higher and you will always be performing at your optimum level

*Always
play
things
how
you
see
fit*

Worrying
doesn't
change
anything
so
don't
do
it

*Be aware
that you
will
have
to
change
for
the
things
that
you
want*

When
you
do
get
your
goals
accomplished
they
begin
to
accumulate
everywhere

*It is an
important
lesson
in
life
to
learn
how
to
agree
to
disagree*

On
the bottom
there are
serpents,
that is why
you should try
your
best to make it
to the top
and
stay
there

Without a plan,
it will be
very-difficult
for you
to
get
anywhere
in
life
that
is
rewarding

*Only when
you
have
their
ear
will
they
choose
to
listen
to
you*

*It is always
important to
have
back-up plans
because
when your best
laid plans
go out the
window,
you will need
to go to your
alternate*

*You should not
only
want to
make it to the
top
but you should
want
to
stay
up-there
as
well*

*Many
different
things
will
come
to you
as
a
byproduct
of
your
progress*

*When
it
doesn't
sound
normal
it
usually
isn't
right*

*Reality
and
theory
are
two
different
kinds
of
friends*

*Over
doing
is
exactly
equal
to
wasting
time*

*What you do
and the
choices that
you make will
dictate
how
the rest
of
your
life
will
become*

*Everyone
in
life
should
have a
dream
that
they
should
follow,
including
you*

*What
you
earned
is
what
you get,
it
is
unethical
to
claim
extra*

*Most times
you
have
to
make
your
own
luck
in
this
world*

*If you make a
hard-bed
eventually you
are going to
have to sleep in
that
hard-bed
so
why not
make
a
soft-one*

*It
is
up
to
you
to
take
care
of
yourself*

*You should
go after
the life
that you
would love
to
live
and not
stop
for anything
until you
get it*

A very important question in your life that you need to ask yourself is; are you following your passions and do you have an active role in it

*When
you set out
to do something
and
you get it
done
there is a
satisfying
feeling of
accomplishment
that comes
with it*

*Whosoever
has
the
money
will
eventually
have
the
power
at
some-point*

Always be careful when you align yourself with someone because you become a part of the same things that their a part-of

*How
can
you
start
to
become
a
better
person
today*

It is extremely
important to
map
before
you
go
and
to
plan
before
you
do

*By the direction
that things
are
currently
heading,
is your
happily ever
after
going to
be
happily ever
after*

*By rushing
through
things
you
tend to
miss
solutions
that
are
right
under
your nose*

*You will
never
know who is
right
for
you
until
you
get
to
know
yourself*

When your
life
gets
slowed
down
you tend to
see
it
for
what
it
really-is

For what you want, you either pay now or you pay later but

in

the end

you

will still

have

to

pay

*Sometimes
it is easier
just to
start
all
over
instead
of
altering
the
existing
project*

The real world, is being forced to learn what you were never taught

*Don't ever
assume
when dealing
with
people
that there
is
some kind
of
thinking
going
on*

*No matter how
drastic or
bad
things get,
there
are
always
standards
that
you
must
uphold*

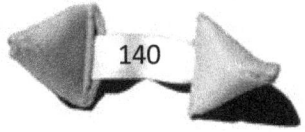

When not paying attention, your progress will have a way of getting away from you

*When you do
what you have
to do to get
where you
have
to
go,
you
will
always
get
there*

*The
most
important
person
that
you
need to
learn
to
listen
to is
yourself*

Things in life
rarely
work-out
as
simply
as
you
want
them too
so don't
get
discouraged

*The best
thing
that you
can
do
for
yourself
is
to
believe
in
yourself*

You
should
never
postpone
what
is
inside
of
you;
get
started

*Certain
people,
you
just
do
not
need
in
your
life*

*You should
always
take
the
opportunity
to
up
the
level
of
your
lifestyle*

*Sometimes it is
only after
we have
lost
everything
that
we
are
free
to
do
anything*

*When your
ego
gets
to
big,
one
day
it
will
explode
all over
you*

*Be smart
enough
to
realize
that
people
do
have
sidebar
conversations
about
you*

*What
seems
like
the
worst
idea
now,
later
can
become
the
best*

*Don't
ever
forget
where
they
were,
when
you
needed
them*

*Only when
you
look
hard
enough
will you
find
what
you
are
searching
for*

*We all
get
treated
exactly
the
way
we
allow
ourselves
to
be
treated*

You have to dream with your efforts in order to make your dreams come true

*It
will
always
pay
to
be
smarter*

Learn
to
use
your
mind
as
if
your
using
a
tool

Sometimes
getting
from
point A
to
point B
is
not
the
point
at
all

The end

Additional books written by
Dr. Kareem Pottinger available online at

www.FORTUNECOOKIES.me

and your local book stores nationwide

FORTUNE COOKIES VOLUMES 1-11

also

available

on

your

Kindle

Nook

Apple

devices